HOW TO DRAW
WITH PEN AND BRUSH

How To Draw

A BOOK FOR

With Pen & Brush

BEGINNERS

by Arthur Zaidenberg

AUTHOR OF "HOW TO DRAW PORTRAITS,"
"HOW TO PAINT IN OIL,"
"HOW TO DRAW CARTOONS," ETC.

New York

THE VANGUARD PRESS

1 9982

INTRODUCTION

Student and professional artists have long found pen and India ink a delightful medium for drawing. Not only is the pen, from the earliest years of schooling, almost as familiar to the hand as the pencil, but it is available everywhere and it is inexpensive. Even without the practice of drawing, almost everyone has acquired skill in the use of the pen through writing. The written word in longhand script is often very beautiful and can be of very intricate design.

Writing a flowing script is in itself a kind of drawing skill—a skill not unlike that required for drawing objects or humans.

In this book I shall demonstrate the uses of the various types of pens and brushes in making drawings with India ink, as well as some of the tools used by the Japanese and Chinese in making their splendid ink drawings.

The methods I teach in these pages are only to be considered a start on your delightful path to becoming an artist.

You may never become a great artist—on the other hand, you may—but you are sure to find pleasure in the use of these materials and you may give much pleasure to others with the work you produce.

India ink is a rich, deep black substance, thicker in body than the ink you use in your fountain pen.

You must be careful not to overload your delicate drawing pen or your fine brush with it, because the heavy ink spreads and makes blots easily and blots are difficult to remove. Many a fine drawing has been ruined by a fat black blot from a carelessly dipped pen.

You can draw or brush or paint with pen and India ink

India ink used with your pointed brush is capable of "saying" things quite different from the pen's lines.

A fine-pointed springy brush in a practiced hand has more "play" than a pen. You are, in fact, painting when you use it.

DRAWING BOARD
WOOD OR
MASONITE

SMOOTH
FINISH
WHITE
DRAWING
PAPER

SOAP
ERASER

BLOTTER

GUM
ERASERS

CLEAN WATER

PENKNIFE

TUBE OF OPAQUE
WHITE

SINGLE-EDGED
RAZOR BLADE

WATER
COLOR
BRUSH

CLEAN RAG

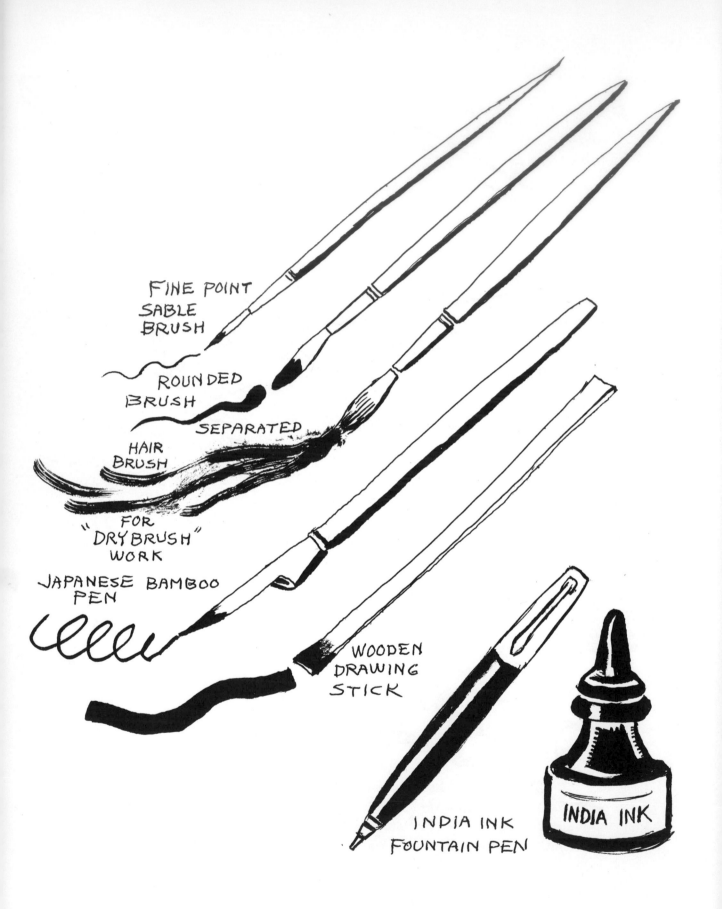

FINE POINT SABLE BRUSH

ROUNDED BRUSH

SEPARATED HAIR BRUSH

FOR "DRY BRUSH" WORK

JAPANESE BAMBOO PEN

WOODEN DRAWING STICK

INDIA INK FOUNTAIN PEN

INDIA INK

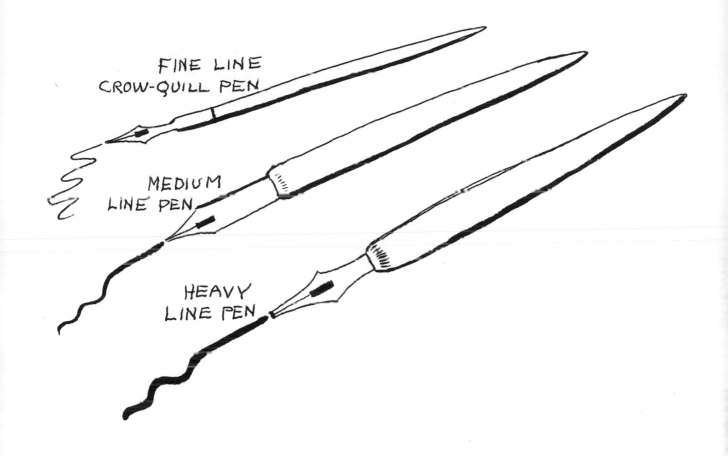

FINE LINE
CROW-QUILL PEN

MEDIUM
LINE PEN

HEAVY
LINE PEN

PENS

The choice of the proper pen for the subject to be drawn is a very important one. Pens with fine points are obviously unsuited to bold, dark drawing. Blunt, heavy pens are unsuited to delicate, fine line drawing.

Pens that are of medium size and quality of point are suitable to most sketching needs.

Pen points are inexpensive. Buy about five points of various size and practice until you find a comfortable tool to suit your special needs.

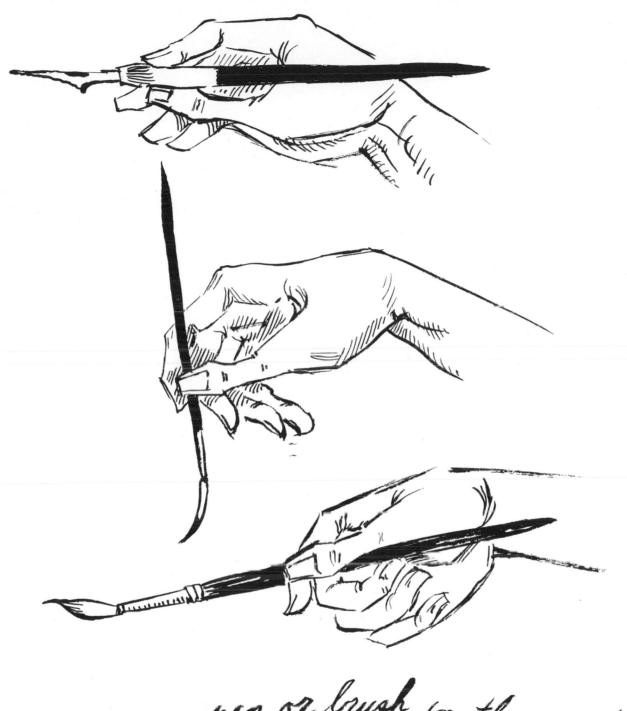

Hold your pen or brush in the most comfortable way for you

PAPER FOR PEN AND INK

Almost any smooth paper can be used for pen and ink except that which is too soft. This would absorb the ink almost like a blotter.

Art supply shops sell inexpensive sheets of paper called "Bristol board." These are made in a choice of two surfaces, kid finish and smooth finish. The smooth-finish Bristol is suggested for very fine line drawings, the kid for freer rough sketches. But remember that any hard-surface paper on which an unblurred line can be drawn is satisfactory for pen and ink drawing.

For brush and ink drawing, a rougher surface with some "tooth" is preferred.

When you draw with pen and ink on smooth-surface paper, avoid the use of a blotter. Let your drawing dry naturally. Blotting grays your lines and may spread them.

It has been said that "the pen is mightier than the sword."

Loaded with India ink, it has had, in the hands of an artist, the power of a cannon. It can also have the delicacy of a needlepoint.

With practice and love, it can become an extension of your sensitive fingers and the messenger of your most subtle ideas.

The range of expression you can obtain with pen and ink is wider than the range you can get with a lead pencil—blacks blacker in rich masses, and lines finer and thinner than any possible with a pencil.

With slight variations of pressure on your pen, it is possible to express any mood you wish when you have become familiar and feel at home with it.

That familiarity can only come with practice.

The exercises shown on the next pages are intended to demonstrate some of the range and quality of pen and ink drawing and also to serve as methods of practice.

Combine several techniques in one drawing.

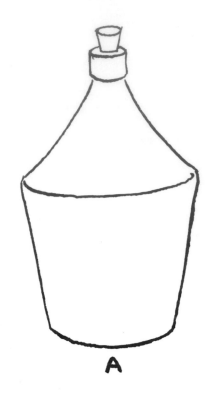

A

FIVE JUGS

Here are five drawings of a jug, using a different pen technique for each one.

Drawing A is drawn entirely in even lines, with no accent on any part of the jug.

Drawing B is drawn in lines of varying thickness. The lines are also "broken." This "lost and found" quality gives the drawing more reality. Look about you and you will see that the edges of things exposed to light and shadow all have that "lost and found" quality. The thicker lines help suggest the light and shade on the jug.

Drawing C is drawn almost entirely in vertical lines. Notice that the parts of the jug nearest to your eye are almost entirely white. This gives an impression of roundness.

Drawing D is more finished, with greater attention to light and shade. Notice that the background and base upon which the jug stands are also drawn, and that the shadows are indicated.

Drawing E is almost the reverse of Drawing D. By indicating the background and leaving much of the jug itself to the imagination, it reveals the jug's curving shape.

B

D

C

E

LINE DRAWING

Line drawing is the use of the single line to outline the boundaries of a form so that it "suggests" the solid three dimensions of an object without shading or drawing the interior details.

Look about you and you will see that nature does not "draw" in line. All objects

are bounded by edges that outline the forms, but the areas within those boundaries are colored and full of detail.

Line drawing is strictly an invention of the artist and it is a very clever one. It is a kind of shorthand drawing, allowing the skillful artist to tell the story of a complex object with a few strokes. If he does it well, he leads the onlooker to fill in all the missing details for himself.

PEN PROBLEMS

Give yourself problems that will challenge your skill and imagination at the same time.

A chair with its wooden legs and rungs will test your ability to "see" in a simple manner the way in which parts of an object appear to be larger when close to the eye and smaller as they recede. This is called "perspective." Notice, too, that the parts closest to your eye are deeper in tone than those farther off. You must try to express that movement in space with your pen.

The softness of the chair cushion will test your ability to give an "impression" with your pen, an impression of the contours and character of the material.

A book with the pages fluttering, an end table with a telephone on it—in short, all the objects around you—are your models and each offers its special problems for you to solve with your pen or brush. You will know you have solved these problems satisfactorily when you can sit back and look at your drawing and say, "That about tells the story of those objects as I see them."

PEN SKETCHES

Many beginners make the mistake of confusing quick sketching with carelessness. Freedom and speed must be accompanied by thought and concentration. A simple sketch, no matter how free from detail, should not be sloppy and crude. In fact, everything in nature is so complex, so full of detail, that it requires thought and good taste in order to make a good, simple sketch of any object.

It is particularly important to sketch frequently with your pen because one of the greatest qualities of pen and ink drawing is its clean, sharp line. Only by long practice can you become so familiar with the drawing pen that your lines will have that quality.

FREE "SCRIBBLE" TECHNIQUES

FORMAL TECHNIQUE

scribble technique

DRYBRUSH

The name "drybrush" is not quite descriptive of this pleasant way of drawing.

The brush is never actually dry.

The process is as follows:

A sable brush, not too fine, is dipped into the ink and then brushed on a practice sheet of paper until the flowing, wet ink is used up and the still damp brush hairs are now spreading and giving strokes of graying lines of an irregular, soft nature.

This quality is highly variable and the drybrush strokes are never exactly uniform. Fortunately, uniformity is not necessary. A drybrush drawing is free and informal in character. It is as playful a way of ink drawing as there is, and its crude, unpredictable quality is part of its charm.

Practice is important in the use of any tool or material, but it is most important in one that is difficult to control, as is drybrush. When used with taste and skill, beautiful, soft drawings can be made this way, with a special quality different from that obtained from any other ink drawing technique.

STICK DRAWING

The use of a stick, either sharpened to a point or used with a broad, blunt end, is older than writing.

Many Chinese and Japanese artists still use a sliver of bamboo dipped in ink as a drawing tool, with delightful results.

Bamboo may not be close at hand for your experiments, but other wood substitutes are available. I have found that the pliant, slim wooden holder of an ice cream pop makes a fine drawing instrument. If you wish to vary the width of the blunt drawing end, the wood may be split into slivers of various widths.

At first you will find this drawing tool crude by contrast with the delicate pen and the soft-yielding brush. But with some practice and play, you will begin to discover the wide range of strokes and flowing broad lines of which the stick is capable.

Study the practice sheet of stick strokes and make several similar playful pages of practice stick drawings. You may find pleasures in the use of the stick that you cannot find in the pen or brush.

These flat stick drawings, made with a quarter-inch-wide, pliant piece of wood, are examples of the basic use of what is a most satisfying drawing tool, capable of a wide range of expression.

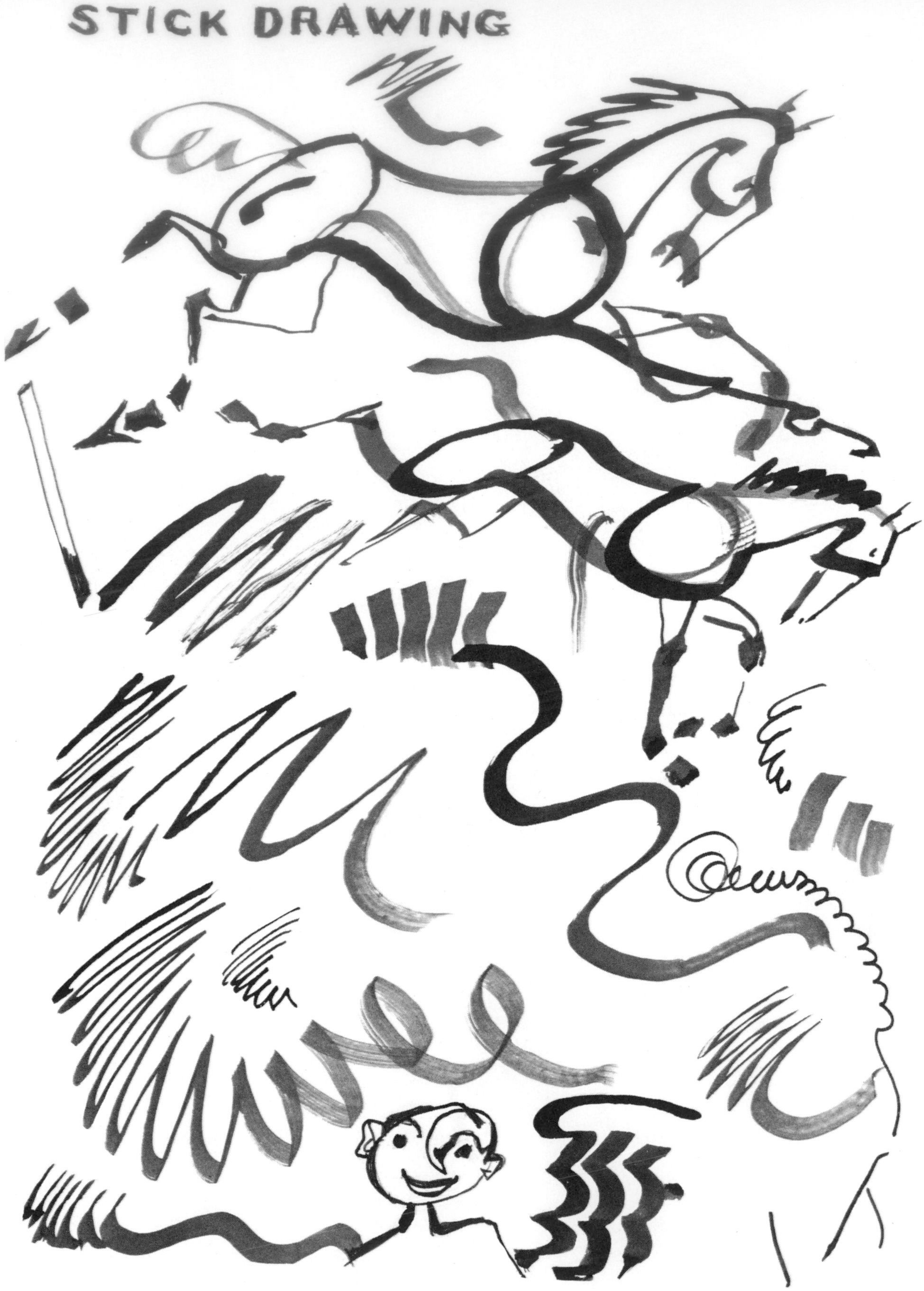
STICK DRAWING

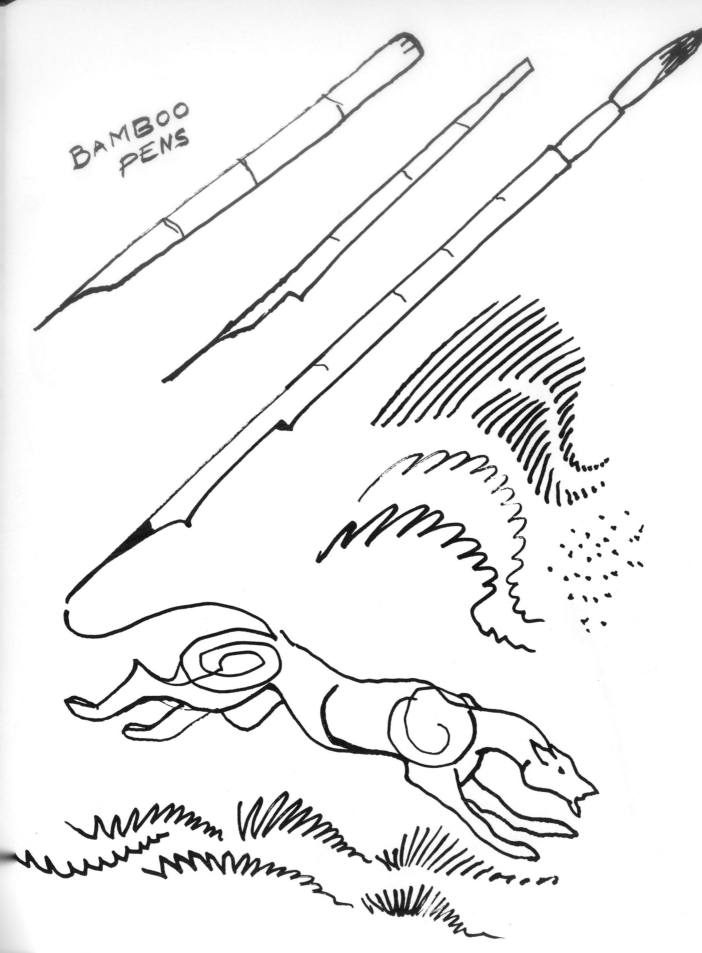

BAMBOO PENS

Bamboo pen sketches

SCRATCHBOARD DRAWING

This is a delightful method of adding to the fun and quality of your pen and ink drawings.

The scratchboard itself may be bought at any art supply store.

It is simply drawing paper covered with a thin coating of smooth, white clay. The name "scratchboard" means just what it says.

When India ink lines or spots are drawn on the clay-surfaced paper, scratches may be made on the black ink with any sharp-pointed tool. The scratches reveal the white surface beneath.

Many people who work on scratchboard like to use a single-edged razor blade, but any sharp pointed or edged instrument will do. A pocketknife makes a fine scratchboard tool.

SCRATCHBOARD

SINGLE-EDGE
BLADE

SCRATCHBOARD

TONES OR VALUES

Pen and ink lines are black, but by combining the pen lines with the white paper surface around them, a wide variation of tones or "values" may be obtained.

Tones are gradations of gray that range from light to dark. Artists call these tones of gray "values."

When pen lines are thin and not very close together in any area on the paper, they produce a light gray value.

When the lines are heavier and closer together, they produce a deeper gray.

The range of possible values is enormous, ranging from almost white to solid black. The values are varied by the quantity and quality of the ink lines used and the amount of white area that is covered or left exposed.

SHADING AND SHADOWS

The amount of shading on an object depends upon the amount of light upon that object and the direction from which the light comes.

When light comes from one side of an object, that side is bathed with the light and the opposite side is in shadow. There is also a shadow cast by the object itself. The shadow falls on the side turned away from the source of light.

TEXTURE

Everything has texture. Texture may be described as the "feel" of the surface to the touch and the nature of its appearance to the eye.

A peach has a unique fuzzy texture; an apple's texture is quite different. A rock has a surface quite different from that of a leaf.

It is not possible to reproduce the texture of all the objects you draw with your pen, but you must be aware of the object's texture and "suggest" that quality to the person who looks at your drawing.

You may simulate the surface grain, its rough or smooth character, its softness or rigidity, by carefully copying the surface details, but the best way—the artist's way—is to try to convey to the viewer the nature of texture by suggestion. Soft lines will express the soft fuzz of the peach surface; smooth, bold lines will describe the cold, hard apple skin; delicately traced lines will suggest the pliant leaf.

FRUIT BOWL SERIES

A bowl of fruit is an excellent subject for the practice of techniques and study of textures.

The first outlines for your drawing in pen and ink should be made very lightly with a sharp-pointed pencil. These preliminary lines will either be erased after you have completed the pen and ink drawing or they will be "lost," made almost invisible by the covering ink lines or by the contrasting strength of ink compared to light pencil lines.

Do not make a "finished" pencil drawing first. The purpose of the pencil drawing is to experiment, to make your mistakes and corrections in a material that is easily erased. Pen and ink corrections require scraping or covering with opaque white paint. The results are messy.

Use a soap eraser to remove the faint pencil lines still visible after you have completed your drawing in ink.

In this series, each drawing of the bowl and fruit has been done in a different pen or brush treatment, and the results are worth studying.

Drawing A of this series was done with a line of even quality, unvaried in its strength. A broad-pointed pen was used.

There was no attempt made to suggest light and shade, three dimensions, or the various weights or textures of the fruit.

The result is a "design," or pattern of the bowl and its contents.

In making Drawing B, the object was to try to express with the use of "drybrush" technique the bulk of the bowl, the contours of the fruit and some suggestion of its texture, and the light and shade upon the whole group. While this drawing is more "realistic" than Drawing A, it is only a mild attempt to depict the actual nature of the object. It is an "impression."

Drawing C, done with a medium pen, is a more detailed study of the play of light on the objects. While still only an impression of the character of the group, the result describes the weight, bulk, and lighting of the whole still life.

Notice that curved lines were used to help express the contour of turning objects. Cross-hatched lines produced the deeper shadows.

Drawing D is the most "finished" drawing of the series. The deep black of the background serves as a frame to the fruit, which is drawn with more detail and texture than the previous three examples.

There is no one rule for judging when a drawing is completely "finished." You must rely on your own good taste and the feeling you get when you have "said" enough about that which you are drawing. Drawing does not require any more natural skill than writing the script you learned in school.

Bob

Fanny Harry Joseph

Tommy Alice Jerry

Philip Adrian James

Arthur

Phoebe Blake Frank

Amy William Gloria

Barry Miriam

Albert Frances

Josephine Othel Peter

George May Tommy Harriet

Edna Helen

Smith

Henry

Florence Harrison

John Green Bill Brown

This tree was "written." Try a few exercises like this simple one. You will find it real fun and good practice.

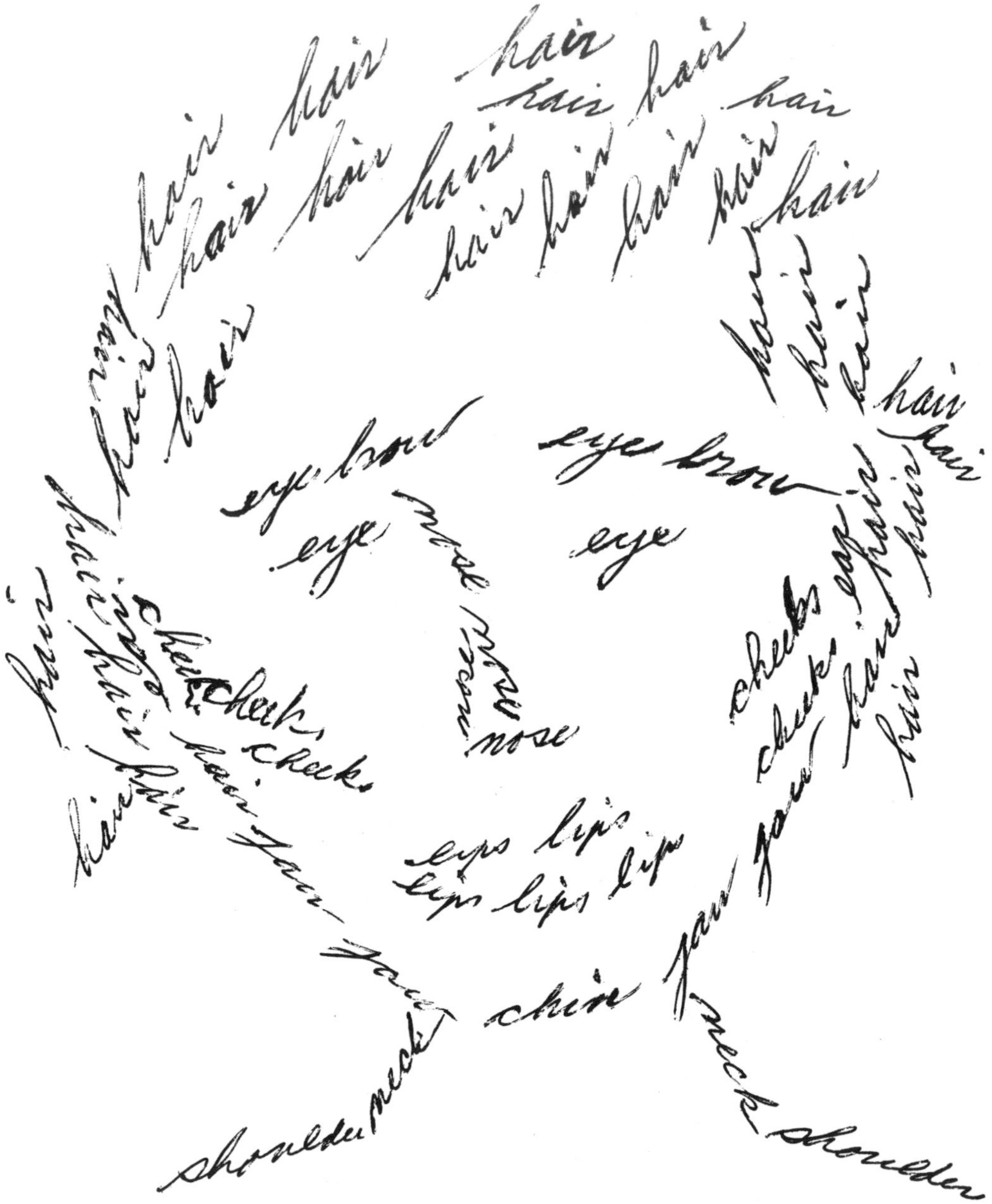

hair hair hair hair hair hair hair hair hair hair hair hair hair hair
hair hair hair hair hair hair hair
eyebrow
eye brow
eye
eye
nose
nose
nose
cheeks
cheeks
cheeks
cheeks
ear
ear
hair hair hair hair hair hair hair hair
lips lips
lips lips lips
jaw
jaw
jaw
jaw
chin
neck
neck
shoulder
shoulder

now try to "write" some
objects or animals - like these

A LAST WORD

In these pages you have been shown some of the many ways to use pens, brushes, and other tools, together with ink. Remember, however, that the best way to learn is by doing. You must practice the exercises shown here and you must make countless drawings in your sketchbook.

In addition, look at beautiful drawings in India ink by fine artists. They will teach you a great deal and give you much pleasure. They will also stimulate your taste and give you ideas for your own creative work.

If you love art, you will begin to think like an artist and it will show in your drawings.

You may become an artist—a good one and perhaps even a great one.

In any event, you will have much pleasure in creating, and you will give much pleasure to those who see your work.

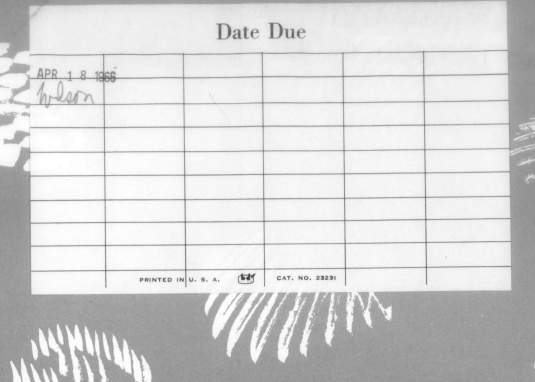